all you need is ...
a whiteboard, a marker and this book!

Book 1

Speaking, Writing and Listening activities
for Pre-Intermediate to Upper Intermediate students

by Matt Potter

Everytime Press ❖ Australia

Published May 2016

Copyright © Matt Potter and Everytime Press

All rights reserved by the author and publisher. Except for brief excerpts used for review or scholarly purposes, no part of this book may be reproduced in any manner whatsoever without express written consent of the publisher or the author.

ISBN: 978-1-925101-82-9

Everytime Press
4 Warburton Street
Magill SA 5072
Australia

Email: sales@everytimepress.com
Website: http://www.everytimepress.com
Everytime Press catalogue: http://www.everytimepress.com/apps/webstore/

Original front cover image copyright © Jay Lopez
(and yes, we know it's a blackboard)
Cover design by Matt Potter

Contents

Introduction / 7

Speaking activities / 9

Speaking ... and Food and Shopping
- Weekly Shopping / 11
- All Aboard Alphabet Airlines / 14
- Dinner Party Plans* / 17
- Buying a Car* / 21
- World's Worst Diet / 24

Speaking ... and Travel
- North and South / 27
- Packing Lightly / 30
- Whirlwind Travel / 32
- Tourist Brochures v. The Real Thing / 34

Speaking ... and Media and Entertainment
- My TV / 38
- Casting a Film / 42
- Song Lyrics / 45
- Film Festival / 48
- Mini-Media Madness* / 50
- Starting a Band / 55

Writing activities / 59

Writing ... and Travel
- Airline Disaster / 61
- Long Plane Trips / 64
- Going through Customs / 66

Writing ... and Food
- The Worst Food I Ever Ate! / 69
- Menu Madness / 72
- Divine Dinner / 75
- Favourite Recipe / 78

Writing ... and Daily Life
- How to Get to My Place / 81
- My Dream Job / 84
- Getting Greener / 86
- What is Polite? And What is Not? / 89

Writing ... and Leisure Time
- Gossip Column / 92
- Film Review / 95
- Rules of the Game / 98
- My Favourite Book ... Not Yet Written / 101

Listening activities / 105

Listening ... and Remembering
- Interpreting / 107
- Memory Lines / 110
- Eavesdropping / 113
- Diplomacy / 116

Listening ... and Describing
- Feeling Your Way #1 / 119
- Feeling Your Way #2 / 122
- Favourite Plot / 125
- Looking Out the Window / 127

Listening ... and Grammar and Vocabulary
- Homophonomania / 129
- Superlative BINGO! / 132
- Cooking BINGO! / 136
- BINGO! for any Topic / 143
- Phrasal Verb Mix 'n' Match / 144
- Human Dictionary / 150
- Seasonal Activity / 156

* These speaking activities require students to gather information outside the classroom, and thus can work well by either providing the class with a break in the formal lesson, or by teaching the activity over two lessons, with the information gathering being given as homework in between.

Introduction

I know from own experience as a relief (or substitute) English as a Second Language teacher, having interesting and relevant activities at your fingertips is a great asset. This is particularly true if you have been called in that morning to teach, and have had no time to plan your lesson/s beforehand.

I also know from my own experience as a relief (or substitute) English as a Second Language teacher, a great resource to have would be a book with activities that are fully contained within the book, on the page: no other resources would be needed, not even copying. You could enter the classroom and all you would need would be a whiteboard, a marker, and the book. No other technology necessary!

Alas, I never found that book.

So I wrote this book.

The activities in this book – which really do require nothing more of you than this book, a marker and a whiteboard – can buy you time in the classroom while you prepare or research other activities. This can be especially important at the beginning of a class.

The activities in this book can also work equally well at the end of a class, when there is some spare time and fun, amusing, imaginative activities are needed.

None of the activities within this book require any preparation on your part beyond reading what the activity is about beforehand. Plus, the activities use the details and stories of students' daily lives, and their talents and opinions. No more alienating stories about people or characters your students will never meet!

This book will not cost you time copying, printing, or searching on the internet, or require other books, DVDs, CDs and CD-ROMs, or indeed anything else.

This book is also very portable!

While the topics for each activity are universal, you may wish to include specific grammar or vocabulary within each activity. Alternate, extra and extension tasks are also offered at the end of each activity.

In our resource rich world, we can come to depend upon technologies to assist us in so many ways, including learning.

To use this book, students will only need paper, a pen and their own abilities.

And beyond your own talents, enthusiasm and time, all you will truly need when using this book, is a whiteboard, and a marker.

Matt Potter, May 2016

Speaking activities

Weekly Shopping

1 Ask students to write down all the items they buy every week or every two weeks, including food, personal toiletries, transport tickets, household goods, cleaning items, etc. (You may have to teach the meaning of <u>household</u>, <u>fortnight</u>, <u>toiletries</u>, etc.)

Students should perform this task on their own.

2 Students feed back their lists to the class. Write each item on the whiteboard, being careful not to make the items too complex (e.g. write <u>eggs</u> rather than one dozen eggs; <u>rice</u> rather than 1 kg rice). Some items will of course be common items.

3 Ask students to then give the amount of money each item costs. Start with those students who speak less frequently in class, as some items will be bought by a number of students. Write the prices against the items on the whiteboard.

4 Put students in pairs. Tell students they are now new housemates or flatmates, and together they have $50 to spend on their joint weekly shopping. Students must negotiate with each other what they may buy, and can only choose items from the list (and their prices) on the whiteboard. They cannot spend more than the agreed amount. To make this easier, student pairs should write down their lists.

5 Each pair feeds back to class, what they bought. Tick each item on the whiteboard as you go. Elicit discussion about the items bought by many, or bought by most but not all. For example, if rice is on the whiteboard but students whose staple food is rice have not chosen to buy rice, ask them to explain why.

6 After each pair has given their choices, tell them you are giving them an extra $50 and they can now choose more items, but again only from the list on the whiteboard.

7 Students negotiate again in their pairs.

8 Each pair again feeds back to the class, what they bought. Tick each item on the whiteboard as you go. Elicit discussion about the items bought again, particularly if the items purchased are unique to that pair e.g. a 'phonecard as opposed to more food.

9 Now tell students you are giving them an extra $50 but this time they can spend it on anything they like, whether on the board or not.

10 Students feed back to class.

Alternate activities

• Restrict students' choices to food only, not toiletries, etc.

• Restrict students' choices to items beginning with certain letters or sounds i.e. only items beginning with A to L, or M to Z, etc.

All Aboard Alphabet Airlines

1 Ask students what sort of cuisine is their favourite food.
Is it Chinese? Italian? Indian? Food from their home country?

2 Put students in pairs. Tell students they are preparing the menu for an eleven hour plane flight from Perth to Cape Town.

3 Tell students: Cape Town is 6 hours ahead of Perth. The plane departs Perth at 10.00am.
It arrives 11 hours later in Cape Town at 3.00pm, Cape Town time, on the same day.

4 Write the chart below on the whiteboard:

	Depart	Arrive
Time in Perth	10.00am	
Time in Cape Town		3.00pm

5 During the 11 hours, students must schedule two meals and a snack for the passengers, drinks included.

Students must choose appropriate airline food, and each food must start with a different letter of the alphabet. None can be repeated.

6 Students feed back their menus to the class. This could lead to a discussion of the issues of long plane flights, including health issues such as Deep Vein Thrombosis (DVT), and how to combat them.

Extra Activity

• Once students have completed the first task, tell them they must work out a schedule for when the meals will be delivered.

Add the figures in italics on the chart below, on the whiteboard:

	Depart	Arrive
Time in Perth	10.00am	9.00pm
Time in Cape Town	4.00am	3.00pm

Students must work out when the food and drinks will be served:
• the time into the flight (how many hours and minutes into the flight)
• the time on the ground in Perth, when the food will be served in the air, and
• the time on the ground in Cape Town, when the food will be served in the air.

Feed back answers to the whole class.

Dinner Party Plans

** This activity requires a visit to a local shop or supermarket, so it could work well as homework.

1 Ask students to think of their favourite recipe or dish.
(You may have to teach the meaning of the word <u>dish</u> in this context.)

Write students' favourite recipes or dishes on the whiteboard, asking the following questions as you do:
• Are these dishes easy to make?
• Do they require cooking, or just preparing? (You may have to teach the difference between <u>cooking</u> and <u>preparing</u> food.)
• Have you ever made this dish yourself? If not, would you be able to find the recipe and make it yourself?

2 Divide students into threes.

Tell students they are all sharing a house or flat and have invited friends over for dinner. Now they must decide the food they will serve.

Each student is responsible for cooking or preparing one course or dish each – it could be savoury or sweet, a starter or the main dish or dessert. Simple dishes will be best, or at least dishes with fewer ingredients. Whatever they choose, it should be inexpensive and nourishing.

It is also important that dishes be as varied as possible. Three dishes all featuring couscous or beef will become boring, as much as some people might like couscous or beef!
(This may be an opportunity for teaching the words and meanings for different courses.)

3 Each student must make a list of all the ingredients for the dish.

(You could leave the remainder of this activity for homework now, if you choose. Students may wish to consult family members or recipe books etc, to complete the activity.)

4 Once their list is completed, tell students they must research the prices for all the ingredients. This will mean a visit to a local shop or supermarket. Tell students that the prices do not need to be exact e.g. if a recipe calls for a teaspoon of salt or two apples, the price of a packet of salt or a kilo of apples is fine.

5 Students must then return to the classroom, and total the price for their individual dishes, then total the price for the entire meal.

6 Each group then feeds back the dishes (no need to go into great detail about the ingredients) and the total price, to the class.

Write these totals for each group, on the whiteboard.

7 Tell the class they must vote for the winner, which should be the group with the greatest variety of (complementary) dishes, for the most economic (or cheapest) price.

Alternate activities

• Tell students it is National Fruit Week and they must include a fruit dish in their dinner menu.

• Tell students there is no way they can cook the food (a power blackout, for example) so the recipes they must choose must be recipes that do not require cooking, only preparing.

Buying a Car

** This activity requires research in local newspapers or on the internet, so it could work well as homework.

1 Ask students what is their dream car. If they do not have a dream car, ask them about the sort of cars they like. If they simply want a car that gets them from A to B, then that is fine too, but they will still need to think about what that car can do.

2 Tell students to write down the features they would want their dream car to have:
• should it have two doors, three doors, four doors or five doors?
• what number of cylinders and engine size should it have?
• what colour should the body and interior be?
• should it have leather or vinyl or cloth seats and trim?
• what overall size should it be: large or medium or small? Should it be a car or a van or even a truck? Will it need to take children, or older parents and other family members, or pets?
• will it need to tow a caravan or trailer?
• how old should the car be – does it have to be new or is second hand OK?

3 Put students in pairs. Tell them they are going to buy a car together that they have to share.

Students must negotiate the sort of car they will buy. It should meet the needs of both students as much as possible.

(You could leave the remainder of this activity for homework now, if you choose.)

4 Tell students they must find a car on the local market that is closest to the car they have decided to buy. They will need to look at local newspapers or on the internet to find this car.

Tell students they can drive up to 100 kilometres (or 60 miles) away to buy the car, but no further. (That is 100 kilometres or 60 miles to the destination and 100 kilometres or 60 miles return.)

5 Students feed back to the class the type of car they were looking for, and the type of car they actually chose.

Ask students if there were any compromises they had to make in deciding which car to look for, and any compromises they had to make (again) when they chose the car they would buy.

Alternate activities

• Tell students they are buying a car for a family member instead, so their criteria may be different.

• Instead of buying a car, use household goods i.e. a new fridge or an oven, etc.

World's Worst Diet

1 Ask students to think about their favourite foods. Students feed back to the class.

Write these on the whiteboard as a list.

2 Repeat as per above, creating three more lists, with:
- foods students really don't like;
- foods students believe are healthy; and
- foods students believe are unhealthy.

3 Compare the four lists and ask students if any foods feature on more than one list.

4 Put students in pairs.
Tell them they are planning to stay home all weekend. All the food they will be eating and the drinks they will be drinking this weekend are unhealthy.
(You may wish to teach the word <u>binge</u>.)

Tell them that starting from Saturday morning, they must plan their unhealthy menu, three meals a day, for the entire weekend. So that is six meals in total:

Saturday breakfast   Sunday breakfast
Saturday lunch   Sunday lunch
Saturday evening meal   Sunday evening meal

Students must also not repeat a food, nor can they use a food that starts with the same letter <u>more than twice</u> i.e. they can have <u>c</u>ake and <u>c</u>hocolate, but they cannot have <u>c</u>ake, <u>c</u>hocolate and <u>c</u>hips.
(You may wish to write <u>cake,</u> <u>chocolate</u> and <u>chips</u> on the whiteboard as an example.)

Or, you may choose to say students cannot use a food that starts with the same sound <u>more than twice</u> i.e. they can have <u>c</u>hocolate and <u>c</u>hips, but they cannot have <u>c</u>hocolate, <u>c</u>hips and <u>c</u>heezels.

5 Once students have completed their unhealthy diet, feed these back to the class.

6 Students must vote on their choice of who would have the worst diet that weekend.

Extra Activity

• If you or the students are feeling especially gluttonous, or you have more time, you may wish to include morning tea, afternoon tea and supper on both days. Remind students that these meals are just a drink and a snack!

North and South

1 Write the alphabet A to Z in capitals on the whiteboard, leaving space beside each letter for the remainder of a name.

2 Ask students to call out the names of cities from around the world, one for each letter. Write these names on the board. Ask questions about each city: have students visited it, what is it known for, what do they know about it?

3 After the list is complete, put students in pairs.

On the whiteboard, write the following:

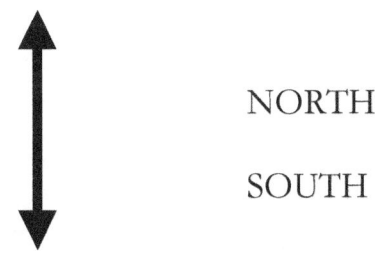

NORTH

SOUTH

4 Instruct students to list the cities from the furthest north to the furthest south and all those in between, in correct order.

(It is not so important that the list be exactly correct, as to prove this may take time and an atlas, but that the students talk about this in English while they perform the task.)

The first pair to complete the list reasonably accurately is the winner.

5 Sorting the list afterwards, as a class on the whiteboard, will elicit further discussion, especially if students disagree.

Alternate activities

• List the cities from closest to furthest from the city or town where your class is being held.

• List the cities from largest to smallest in population.

• List cities west to east, instead.

Packing Lightly

1 Put students in pairs.

Tell students they are going on a short holiday, four days and three nights, together.

Each pair can only take along a small suitcase that they must share. Because the case is small, they can only take 11 items of clothing or other items each, a total of 22 items. (This does not include food or other toiletries.)

2 Students must negotiate with their partners what they will pack for their holiday. They may decide to share items e.g. a large folding umbrella, which they can both use, which counts as one item, instead of 2 smaller umbrellas, which will count as two items.

Note: a pair of shoes = 2 items, and a pair of socks = 2 items

3 Students feed back the lists to the class.

4 The winner could be the pair who has made their list go the furthest.

Alternate activities

• Instead of packing clothes, etc, students choose food items.

• Students choose items that only begin with letters within a certain range i.e. A to H, M to T, etc.

• Students cannot choose items that start with the same letter (beyond paired items, e.g. socks, shoes).

Whirlwind Travel

1 Ask students about any holiday / vacation / travel destinations they would like to visit. This may include places they have already visited, or places they have never been before.

Write them on the whiteboard.

2 Ask students to write down 5 places they would like to visit. These places could be anywhere in the world. Students write these on their own.

3 Put students in pairs. Tell them they are travel partners, and from their list of 5 places each (10 in total) they must choose 7 places they will visit together.

But the catch is that all their travel must be done in two weeks! So together they must negotiate and plan to visit 7 places, spending at least a day in each place, flying (or travelling by the quickest transport possible) between destinations. On Day 15, they must land back at their original destination.

4 Feed back travel itineraries to the class.

Alternate activities

• Students choose only places that start with the same letter.

• Students chose only places that start with different letters, never the same letter.

Tourist Brochures v. The Real Thing

** This activity works best with students who are studying English while living away from their home country.

1 Put students in groups of 3 or 4.

Ask them, what did they hear or know about the city they are now living in, before they arrived?

Were there tourist brochures with beautiful pictures that promised a wonderful and interesting life?

Or did they promise a quieter place that would make studying easy?

What made them choose this city or town rather than other places?

What did they think would be here before they arrived?

2 Ask students to discuss this in their groups and they must write down their points.

3 Each group feeds back their list to the class. Write these on the whiteboard. Issues that come up more than once can be given extra ticks.

4 Now ask students, what is the reality? Is the city or town they have moved to the same as they heard or were promised? How is it different? Is it better or worse?

5 Students discuss this again, writing down their points.

6 Each group feeds back their list to the class.

7 Re-divide the class and put students in pairs again, ensuring that as many students as possible are paired with a student from another group.

8 Tell students they are writing the text for a small tourist brochure for the city or town they are living in now. But this brochure must be truthful! Their brochure must include what the place is really like, not what the tourist brochures or recruiting agents usually say.

The length of the text can be 50 to 150 words, and will depend on how quickly you want to complete this activity and the skill level of the class.

9 Students write the text together, negotiating what will be included.

10 Once complete, students read out their texts to the class.

11 If you want a winner, it could be the text that includes the most information. Or the text that is the most honest. Or the text that sounds most like a real tourist brochure despite its (perhaps) negative images.

Extra activity

• In their groups, students write an acrostic for the city or place they are currently living in, using different adjectives.

P Pretty

A Attractive

R Roaring

I Intellectual

S Summery

My TV

1 Ask students to think about their favourite TV show.

2 Going around the class, ask each student to tell the class what his or her favourite TV show is.

Each student may have more than one favourite show.

If the shows are not known by many students, students may have to explain or describe the show or shows.

Ask students to explain why they like these shows, and who do they think the shows are popular with: older or younger people? Men or women?

Students may also have a favourite TV show genre, and these may be brought up too – crime shows, police dramas, quiz shows, cooking shows, lifestyle shows, talent shows, reality shows, current affairs, etc.
(You may have to teach the meaning of some of these show genres i.e. <u>current affairs</u>. Indeed, you may have to teach <u>genre</u> too, if you use it.)

3 Put students in pairs.

4 Draw the chart below on the whiteboard. You may wish to include half hour slots as well.

Time	TV Show name	Genre or Type	Brief Description
Midnight			
1.00am			
2.00am			
3.00am			
...			
11.00pm			

5 Tell students that using the chart on the whiteboard, they must design programming for a TV station of their choice, for one day, from midnight to midnight. The day of the week is their choice – remind students that weekend programming is often different from weekday programming. Students can use the TV shows from the whiteboard, or use others they may know.

Pairs must negotiate their programming and make sure their own choices are included.

6 Once all the students have finished, students feed back the programme schedules to the class.

This could lead to discussions about sex and violence on TV, and also about the projected audience at different times of the day – children's programming, adult programming, daytime programming, late night programming, etc.

Alternate activities

• Rather than TV shows over 24 hours, students choose leisure activities (including sport) over a 12 or 6 hour period.

• Rather than shows they themselves like, students chose TV shows that a friend or family member would like.

Casting a Film

1 Ask students to think of their favourite actor or actress. (Students may need to have another favourite in reserve.)

2 Ask students to write down five adjectives describing their actor or actress. Also ask about the kind of role their favourite specialises in or usually plays. (This will be especially important if a student chooses an actor or actress not well known outside his or her own country or culture.)

3 Ask each student to name their favourite actor or actress, and write these names on the whiteboard, with their five adjectives and the kind of role they specialise in or usually play. There must be one favourite actor or actress listed for each student in the class.

4 Put students in pairs, and tell them they must come up with a basic plot or story for a film. Students must write a paragraph, four or five sentences long. This may be the plot from a film they have seen recently, or is from one of their favourite films.
(You may have to teach the meaning of plot.)

5 Each pair must then come up with a character or part, as per their plot or story, for each of the actors and actresses listed on the whiteboard. They can be bit parts or major parts.

If the list of favourite actors is too long or onerous, you may want to divide the list of favourites into two or three and divide the pairs in the class similarly. You may wish to assign groups from the whiteboard to pairs of students or allow them to choose themselves.

6 At the end, each pair feeds back their plot and cast list to the class.

7 The class votes as a whole as to which pair's film is likely to be the biggest hit.

Alternate activities

• Students devise the plot together as a class, each student contributing a sentence or plot development in turn. Write these on the whiteboard. The whole class then discusses who should be cast in which role in the film, and why.

• Ask students who their favourites are and why. Then get students to think of who in the class is most like these actors and actresses. Students can either work as a class, or work in pairs.

Song Lyrics

1 Ask students what is their favourite song. Ask them to think about the words, or lyrics.
Are the lyrics important?
Are the lyrics the reason they like the song so much?
Or are they less important than the way the music sounds?

2 Ask students to think about words they commonly hear in songs. Brainstorm these words until 20 words are listed on the whiteboard. Words that rhyme are helpful.

3 Ask students to think about words they never or rarely hear in song lyrics. Brainstorm these words until 10 are listed on the whiteboard. Again, words that rhyme are helpful.

4 Put students in pairs.

Give students a timeframe – 15 minutes, less or more depending upon their language skill level – and tell them to write the lyrics to a song, to include as many of the words on the whiteboard as possible.

It might be helpful to tell students to think of it like a poem, or to think of a song they like, to which they can rewrite the words.

5 The first pair to finish and to include the most words (in a coherent manner) is the winner.

Extra activity

• Ask students to swap their completed lyrics with another pair. Students must choose / highlight 15 alternate words from these new lyrics. Ask students to swap again with yet another pair. Students must now write new lyrics and must include this second set of words.

Film Festival

1 Ask students, individually, to write down the names of five films they like.

2 Put students in pairs.

Student A describes to Student B what he / she likes about each of the films he / she has chosen. Students should take turns describing each film. (Student A then Student B then A then B, etc.)

3 Tell pairs they are joint directors of a small film festival and they must choose five films from their joint list of ten.

Students must discuss which five of the ten films to choose and which to discard. Their final choice must be as disparate or different as possible: five action films starring the same actor will not be accepted!

4 Pairs feed back their final choices to the class.

5 The class votes for the Film Festival they think is the best.

Alternate activity

• Instead of favourite films and a film festival, ask students to choose their 5 favourite foods. These foods must then be presented to the class as a meal ... the winner is whose food is the most nutritious, or most delicious, or the cheapest, etc.

Mini-Media Madness

** This activity is great in longer classes when energy in the class is low and a break is called for. Combine the tasks given out with the break. This activity also works best when newsagents and / or newspaper sellers are nearby.

The actual tasks do not take long, but with the break in between, the activity can be extended.

Most of the speaking is done at the beginning of the activity, and at the end when the students report back to the class.

1 Ask students if they read any magazines or newspapers.

Do they read them every time they are published i.e. daily if the newspaper is published daily, or weekly if the newspaper or magazine is published weekly?

Do they read them less often? Why?

Are newspapers and magazines better in their own country? Are there more choices at home?

Do they still regularly read newspapers and / or magazines in their own language i.e. media in other languages is also published in English-speaking countries. Do they read these newspapers or magazines?

2 Students feed back their reading preferences as a class. These do not need to be written on the whiteboard.

3 Then give out the following tasks, one per student. Students may wish to write these down as you tell them.

Students must find out:

1. Whose photo is on the front page of today's local daily newspaper?

2. Who is on the front cover of a golfing magazine?

3. What is the name of a women's magazine?

4. What is the main headline on the front page of today's local daily newspaper?

5. What is the name of a football magazine?

6. Which company publishes a national daily newspaper?

7. What is the number of the last page of today's local daily newspaper?

8. What is the name of a television magazine?

9. Which company publishes the local daily newspaper?

10. Whose photo is on the front page of a national daily newspaper today?

11. What is the main headline on the front page of a national daily newspaper today?

12. Who is on the front cover of a women's magazine?

13. What is the name of a body-building magazine?

14. On which page would you find the comic strips or cartoons in a national daily newspaper?

15. Who is on the front cover of a football magazine?

16. What is the name of a golfing magazine?

17. What is the address of the publisher of the local daily newspaper?

18. Who is on the front cover of a television magazine?

19. What is the number of the last page of a national daily newspaper today?

20. Who is on the front cover of a body-building magazine?

21. What is the colour of the masthead of the local daily newspaper?

22. What is the address of the publisher of a national daily newspaper?

23. On which page would you find the comic strips or cartoons in a local daily newspaper?

24. What is the name of a non-English language newspaper?

25. What is the colour of the masthead of a national daily newspaper?

(You may need to teach the meaning of <u>masthead</u>.)

4 Once the students are all assembled back in the classroom, students should feed back the information they gathered to the class.

Ask students how and where they got the information from.

Be aware that students may all have used the same newsagent or newspaper seller to gather their information, so you may wish to send them out at staggered times, or in different directions.

Alternate activities

• Students devise their own list of information to find.

• Send some of the class out to search for the answers on one day, and the rest of the class on another day, and time each team. The winners are those who take less time to get all the facts correct.

Starting a Band

1 Brainstorm the favourite types or genres of music students in the class like. Write these on the board. (You may also need to teach the word <u>genre</u>.)

If there are many types, you may have to take a vote and only use the most popular types or genres.

2 Divide the class into groups of 3 or 4. Or, if there is an even spread, you may divide the class into groups using their favourite music as a decider.

Tell students each group has come together to form a band.

Each group must decide and negotiate:
• which instruments the band needs to play the type of music it wants to;
• which band members will play which instruments. Some students may already play these instruments in real life; and
• a name for their band.

Individual students must justify their reasons for wanting to play the instrument/s they choose.

3 Each group feeds back to the class the name of their band and which members will play which instruments.

4 Tell students that each group (or band) must now decide the songs it will record for its debut album.
(You may need to teach the word debut.)

Give each group a limit of 10 or 12 songs. They obviously cannot be original songs, but songs already recorded and published.

5 Each group feeds back to the class their song list for their debut album.

Alternate activities

• Make this activity more amusing by telling students to include some songs they dislike.

• Make this activity more amusing by telling students to include only songs they dislike.

Writing activities

Airline Disaster

1 Ask students to think about their experiences with airlines.
Have these experiences always been pleasant?
Are there any airlines they would recommend? Or not recommend?

2 List all the airlines they would recommend on the whiteboard.

3 Ask students what are some of the things that can go wrong while you are flying in a plane, especially a long-distance flight?
Make sure students do not include only plane crashes, but also bad food, bad customers, bad service, bad passengers seated next to you, screaming children, health issues, etc. They may also include things that have happened on the ground: at the airport before or after a flight.

4 List these on the whiteboard.

5 Ask students to write half a page on something that could go wrong on a plane. It could be anything: though it would be useful if not all of them involved crashes!

Tell students not to write about the solution to the problem, as that will come later.

Perhaps students have their own stories from their own experience they can write about.

6 Once students have completed their half a page, tell them to swap their papers with other students, and to read the other students' work.

7 Now tell each student to imagine they are a member of the cabin crew on a plane. And they must write about how they would solve or cope with the problem they have just read about, as that staff member. Obviously, the staff member they choose to be must have some relation to the problem: a pilot is not going to have to deal with a passenger who is snoring too loudly and keeping the other passengers awake!

8 Ask each student to write another half a page, to complete a full page.

9 Once students have finished writing, they should read out the problem they were presented with, and their own solution.

Extra activity

- Ask students to write down the food they had on this flight ... if they can remember it!

Long Plane Trips

1 Ask students what is the longest plane trip they have ever taken.
Did they enjoy it?
Where did the flight start and where did it finish?
How long was it?
And which airline?
What did they do to while their time away?
(You may have to teach the meaning of the term <u>to while away time</u>.)
What are some the hazards of long plane flights?

2 Ask students to write down what they did on this long plane flight.

Tell them to write the text as if it is a set of friendly instructions, a guide from an airline, to its passengers, about ways to make their flight as pleasant as possible.

Agree on a word or time length before starting.

Extra activity

• Ask students to write down things they do when they are whiling away time.

Going through Customs

** This topic will work best when you are teaching people English in a country not their own. However, it can work anywhere: just be mindful that not all students in your class may have travelled to other countries.

1 Ask students what was their first impression of the country where they are living now ... or a country they have visited.

What was the airport like?

How were they treated while going through Customs? Were they shocked or surprised at what happened ... or what did not happen?

Was their luggage searched?

Do they think they would have been treated differently if they had worn different clothes? Or if they had looked different?

2 Ask students to describe how they looked and what they were wearing the last time they walked through Customs in a country not their native country.

3 Ask them to write this description, 100 words or so.

4 Ask students to swap their papers with another student, then to imagine they are working for Customs as a Customs Officer.

How would they treat this person whose description they have just read?

Would they let them continue through Customs without being searched ... or would they search them?

5 Ask students to write what they would do, and to give reasons why, another 100 words or so.

6 Each student should read aloud their own original text, and then the person who is the Customs Officer should read the second text in response to the first.

Extra activity

• Ask students to write down a list of the things they brought with them when they moved to this country.

The Worst Food I Ever Ate!

1 Write the alphabet, A to Z, in columns down the whiteboard.

2 Tell students you want them to think of as many negative adjectives as possible. As they call them out, write them against the letters the adjectives begin with. You will probably find you have multiples for some letters, and none for others.

3 Once the list is complete (i.e. the students have exhausted themselves or you feel it is time to move on), ask students to think about the worst food they have ever eaten.

What did they eat?
Where did they eat it?
Was it for a special occasion?
Who cooked it?
Why was it bad?

4 Now ask students which words would they use to describe this food, and write these on the whiteboard.

Start a quick discussion about this food, then tell students to write an agreed number of words (you decide how long) on the worst food they have ever eaten.

5 Students should include details as per the questions above, and others you asked.

Alternate activity

• Instead of the worst food students have ever eaten, turn the activity around and make it about the best food they have ever eaten.

Menu Madness

1 Ask students what their favourite food is.

Write these on the whiteboard.

If students have more than one each, write them all on the whiteboard.

2 Write the following headings on the whiteboard: Savoury, Sweet, and Snack.
(You may have to teach the meaning of <u>savoury</u>.)

With the students' assistance, place each favourite food under the appropriate heading.

3 Now ask students to think of eating in a local café or restaurant.

Ask them:
Do they have a favourite restaurant or café?
How many courses can they buy or choose?
What are these courses called?
What sort of food is included in these courses?
How big are the servings in these courses?
Are the courses different in a restaurant or café in their own country?

As students respond to these questions, write their answers on the whiteboard.

4 Tell students to imagine they own a restaurant or café and are devising the menu. The menu should include three courses – or starter, the main dish, and dessert – and three choices for each course.

Students may also include three drinks, on a separate list.

The choices do not have to be complicated, and students may wish to have side dishes also. The food can be from their own culture, or from another.

5 After students have devised their full menus, ask them to put a price they believe would be accurate, against each dish.

Extra activity

• Ask students to select one dish each from the three courses, and write down why they think the three dishes would work well together as a complete meal.

(You may have to explain the different meaning of the words complement and compliment.)

Divine Dinner

1 Ask students who, more than anyone, would they like to meet.
It might be a sportsperson or a film star, a political leader or a celebrity or someone from the past. Each student should choose one – unless the class is really small.

Write the names of these people on the whiteboard.

2 Ask students, why would they want to meet them? What would they talk about?

3 Then ask students who of the people they would like to meet, would they invite for dinner, to their home or for dinner elsewhere.

4 Students must choose four guests, but all guests must be people they do not know and would normally not meet in their everyday lives.

Ask students to write these names down.

5 Now ask students which three students in the class would they invite for dinner. These would also be imaginary guests for a dinner party, either at home or elsewhere.

Students write the names of these three fellow classmates down, to complete a list of seven guests. The eighth person is him or herself.

6 Now tell students that you want them to work out a seating plan i.e. who of the guests will sit next to each other. This includes the four famous people, the three classmates, and the student who is the imaginary host.

7 Draw a quick diagram on the whiteboard, of a table overhead, with 8 places for diners.

8 Students should draw a seating plan and name a space for each guest, including themselves. Students should consider the interests and personalities of all their guests.

9 Once students have drawn their plan, students must write a short paragraph on each of the guests, and why the host has chosen to sit each guest where he / she has. Again, students should consider the interests and personalities of all their guests

Alternate activity

• Put students in pairs. Students must negotiate with each other over the seating plan. Note this will become more of a speaking activity by doing so.

Favourite Recipe

** You could kick-start this process by talking about your own favourite recipe.

1 Ask students what is their favourite recipe or dish.

Have they prepared or cooked it?
Have they watched someone else prepare or cook it?
Do they know how to prepare or cook it?
What are the ingredients?
(You may have to teach the meanings of <u>prepare</u> and <u>cook</u>.)

2 Ask students to write down the list of Ingredients. Remind students that the list should include spices and seasonings (including salt and pepper) and liquids including water and pre-prepared broths and soups, etc.

If students do not know the complete list, get them to write down as much as they can remember … or get them to choose a recipe they do know.

3 Once they have completed their list, ask students to write down the Method. (You may have to teach the meaning of <u>method</u>.)

Writing both the Ingredients and the Method can be made easier by writing them as dot or numbered points.

Extra Activity

• Ask the students to make the recipe they have chosen, and bring it to class for a shared meal.

How to Get to My Place

1 Ask students to think of words that are used when giving directions.

Write these words on the whiteboard.

The list may include the following words, and more besides:

metre	mile	feet
distance	kilometre	tram
drive	speed	bus
street	limit	train
road	catch	bike
turn	station	veer
corner	travel	steer

2 Ask students to think of how they would give directions to another student, from the classroom to their home.

What would they say?

3 Ask students to write down these directions.

You may want students to write the directions in paragraphs, though dot points or numbered points would be easier.

You may also want students to include leaving the classroom in their instructions, or you may want them to start from the front of the building.

4 Once students have finished, gather their papers together, mix them up and get students to read aloud other students' directions.

You should hopefully be able to gauge whose directions are complete – or can be followed – and whose are not, as they are being read aloud.

Alternate activity

• Conduct this activity in reverse i.e. ask students to think of how they would give directions to another student, from their home to the classroom.

My Dream Job

1 Ask students if they have ever had paid employment. If so, what jobs have they had?

Write these on the whiteboard.

2 Ask students to describe what makes a job good. And what makes a job bad?

Write these on the whiteboard, as two lists.

3 Now ask students what would their dream job be. If they could have any job in the world, what would it be, and why?

As students will need to write about this job at some length (decide how long), it is a good idea for them to be as realistic as possible. Declaring they wish to be an astronaut may not be very workable, if they really do not know much about what being an astronaut actually involves.

4 Ask students to write about this job. They should consider working hours, pay rates, colleagues, conditions etc, and any other positives about the job.

Extra activity

• Ask students to write about the negatives, or parts of the job they might like less, or not like at all.

Getting Greener

1 Ask students to think about what it is they do every day, on a regular basis.
It might involve going to English lessons or going to their workplace, and it would no doubt involve food purchasing or preparation, travel or transport, etc.

Write these on the whiteboard.

2 Now ask students to list all the things they do, on their own paper, in the order they do them, starting with when they get out of bed in the morning. You might tell them 'til 10.00pm, or lunchtime, or …

3 Ask students what are the ways we can all help the environment.

Write these on the whiteboard.

4 Ask students to write down ways they could do what they do every day, but in a greener, more environmentally way.

They should write these in paragraph form.

This could be only turning on one light – or using more energy efficient light bulbs – or having shorter showers or not having a cooked breakfast and saving on power. This could be car pooling or taking public transport, etc.

Give students a suitable time frame or word length.

5 After students have completed this task, ask them (or some of them, depending upon the class size) to read aloud what they have written.

Extra activity

• Ask students to turn the paragraph they wrote (of things they could do every day to be greener or more environmentally friendly) into a list. Start with most effective and finish with least effective.

What is Polite? And What is Not?

** This activity works best with people studying English in a country that is foreign to them. Otherwise, students will need to think about the language of politeness in English, and in their native language.

Politeness differs from culture to culture. Some cultures find English-language speaking cultures overly polite – we are the ones who often apologise when someone steps on our toes! – yet other cultures find English-language speaking communities too informal.

Formality and informality, are in fact quite different things from politeness and impoliteness.

1 Ask students to think of the basic rules of politeness in their own country.

Are they the same as the country in which they are studying?
How are they different?

Are there ways of being polite, in English, that they think are silly or difficult to understand?

Are there ways of being polite, in their own language, that they think are silly or difficult to understand?

2 Ask students to write a list of basic rules for polite behaviour from their own country. Agree on a number of points: 8 or 10 will get them thinking!

3 Then ask students to write the same for the English language culture they are living in, opposite the points about their own culture.

Do they match? Are they much the same?

Or are they completely different?

4 This could promote further discussion if students are from a variety of different cultures.

Extra activity

• Ask students to write down some informal expressions and their more polite equivalents, or vice versa.

Gossip Column

** Some students may find this exercise culturally embarrassing, so be careful!

1 Ask students if they read gossip magazines, in their own language or in English. This should include entertainment magazines, women's magazines, tabloid magazines, etc.
(You may need to teach the meaning of gossip, tabloid, etc.)

2 Ask students what sort of gossip stories appear in these magazines.

What are their favourite stories?
Whose lives do they follow in these magazines?
Are the stories true?
Can they tell the difference between true stories and untrue stories?
Is gossip true?

Write the article or story themes students identify, on the whiteboard.

3 Now ask students to identify their favourite celebrity. This may be a sportsperson, film star, singer, politician, etc.

If they do not have a favourite, ask students to choose someone.

4 Ask students to imagine a gossip item or article that would include their favourite celebrity ... and themselves. Tell them to write a short article about the two of them: the theme is their own choice – unwanted pregnancy, clandestine love affair, embezzled money, shoplifting, etc.

Give students a word limit, depending upon their ability.

5 Once the articles have been written, get students to read aloud their articles. As mentioned earlier, these could prove funny ... or embarrassing.

Alternate activity

• Ask students to write an article on the time they met their favourite celebrity. Give students a time or word limit, depending upon their ability.

Film Review

1 Ask students what sort of films do they like.

Do they have favourite actors or directors or genres? (You may have to teach the meaning of <u>genre</u>.)

What is their favourite film?

How do students decide whether to see a film or not? Advertising? Reviews? Word of mouth? (You may have to teach the meaning of <u>word of mouth</u>.)

What do students look for in a film? What makes a film good to them?

Write these words or phrases on the whiteboard.

2 Now ask students what are the individual things that make up a film.

Write these on the whiteboard.

Below are some suggestions:
- performances (the actors)
- story and script
- cinematography

- design (the way the film looks, including colour, sets, costumes, locations, etc)
- music and sound, etc

3 Ask students what their favourite film is again. If they do not have a favourite film, get them to choose one they really like.

4 Ask students to write a review of their favourite film, or the one they chose. Decide on a word-length that is appropriate.

Students should include a review of those elements listed on the whiteboard, as well as their general feeling about the film i.e. why they really like it.

Alternate activity

• Instead of their favourite film, ask students about their favourite TV show. Their favourite show may well have been viewed on the internet rather than TV.

Rules of the Game

1 Ask students which sports do they like.

Do they still play them? Have they ever played them? How often?

Write these sports on the whiteboard.

2 If students do not have a sport they like, do they like playing other games?
This could be a computer game or other electronic game or even a board game.

Write these on the whiteboard also.

3 Ask students what the point or aim of the game or sport is.

How does the winner become the winner?
How long does the game – or can the game – last?
How many people play on a team, if it is a team sport?
Is it played in summer or winter … or any season?
What are the most important rules?
And what are the key facts you need to know to understand the game?

4 Ask students to write these important facts and rules down, and finish with a brief explanation (you choose the word count) of their own involvement with the sport or game.

Alternate activity

• Instead of games or sports they like, ask students about sports they don't like.

My Favourite Book ... Not Yet Written

1 Ask students what books do they like to read.

If they do not read books (or even magazines) ask them why.
What would they like to read about?
What would make them read books more often ... or at all?
Is book reading a big part (or any part) of their own culture, or family life?

2 Ask students what they believe are important things or elements a good book should contain or include.

Do they have examples? Which books are they?
Do they know the authors?
Do they have favourite authors who write the sort of books they like to read?

Write these on the whiteboard.

3 Now ask students to write a short or abridged version of the story they would like to read.

(You will probably need to teach the meaning of <u>abridged</u>.)

Agree on a word or page length before students start writing.

Alternate activity

• Put students in pairs. Student A talks about the story she prefers, while Student B talks about the story he prefers.

Student B writes the story that Student A speaks about, while Student A writes the story that Student B speaks about.

Listening activities

Interpreting

1 Ask students what they think would be the problems they might encounter when interpreting speech for another person.

Have they ever interpreted for a family member or friend?
Was it difficult?

What was the situation? At a medical appointment or with a government department, etc?

2 Tell students they must speak for three minutes (or more) on a topic of their choice. It can be about anything they like, but it must be about a topic they know something about.

(Students can make notes on the topic beforehand if they wish.)

3 Ask two students to stand in front of the class. Student A will be speaking about his / her topic to the class.

While this is done, Student B acts like an interpreter for Student A. So Student B must listen to Student A, and then relay the same information to the class, like an interpreter would, but instead the only language spoken by both students should be English.

Student B may paraphrase what Student A says, but must get the meaning of Student A's speech across to the class. Therefore, Student B must use language that is similar but not exactly the same. It should not be verbatim.

Remind Student A that he / she must allow time for Student B, through the course of the speech, to 're-interpret' what A has just said, to the class. Otherwise, Student A will speak for 3 minutes and then Student B will be expected to 'interpret' for the same amount of time, which would be difficult. So a sentence or two or three at a time works well.

4 After they have finished, Student B now speaks on his / her topic while Student C interprets the speech.

Continue this activity through the class until all students have performed both roles, and Student A (the very first student) has interpreted for the final student.

Alternate activity

• Instead of interpreting around the class like a chain, get students to work in pairs. Student A and Student B reverse roles, with Student B speaking and Student A interpreting.

Memory Lines

** This activity works better with larger classes.

1 Write the date on the whiteboard, but write it two ways i.e. the U.S. way (2.17.16 – month first) and the U.K. / European way (17.2.16 – day first.)

Ask students which date is correct, and which one is used in which English-speaking countries.
Which version is used in their own countries?

2 Tell students to line up in order of their birthdays, from January 1st to December 31st. Students must of course use English to negotiate the order in which they should stand.

Check that all students are in the correct month and day order.

3 Starting with January 1st and ending with December 31st, ask each student the month and day of their birthday. Make the whole line repeat aloud each new date, after each individual says his or her birthday. Work down the line from first to last. Students must listen for each month and day. If you have 20 students, this will be done 20 times.

4 Take the first student with the first birthday and ask him / her to say <u>the month</u> of each successive student's birthday, from January to December, down the line. The student must include his / her <u>own month,</u> in the correct order.

Do this with every student down the line. (You will no doubt have repeated months.) Students must include their own month in the correct place.

5 Repeat the exercise but this time include <u>the month and the day</u>. Each student must repeat all the days and months correctly.

If you want a winner, the winner is the student who gets the most dates correct without prompting.

Alternate activities

• Work up the line from the last student / last date, to the first.

• You can repeat this activity with a variety of other themes, though make sure there is more than one fact for students to remember about their classmates: month / day / age; then month / day / age / eye colour, etc.

You could include as many facts about each student as far as time and interest (and memory) allow.

Other topics could include:
• suburb or area where they live now, and the same in their home country;
• their favourite colour and an article of clothing they like to wear in that colour;
• their shoe size and a favourite pair of shoes they like to wear;
• their favourite sport, pastime or hobby and how many years they have been playing or doing it, etc.

Eavesdropping

1 Ask students if they have ever listened to a conversation that they were not a part of.

Where was it? On the bus?
At the train station?
In a queue or line?
(You may have to explain the spelling and meaning of queue.)

Did the people who were having the conversation know he / she was listening?

What are the social rules about listening to other people's conversations in their own cultures?

What would happen if the other people were talking about a problem or had a question, and you butted in and gave them a solution or an answer?
(You may have to explain the meaning of butt in.)

2 Teach students the meaning of eavesdropping.

3 Divide students into threes, and then in each trio, label one Student A, and the others Student B and Student C.

In each group, Students A and B have a conversation (give them a topic or they can choose one for themselves) while Student C listens to their conversation.

Depending upon students' abilities and the length of the conversation, Student C can either take notes and report back after the conversation is finished, or report on the conversation while it is occurring. This latter version would require breaks in the conversation.

Students could perform these tasks in front of the whole class, a group at a time.

4 Or, students could perform these tasks all at the same time, and then Student C from each group, in turn, reports back to the class.

Given time, you can rotate students so every student reports to the class at least once each.

Alternate activities

• Give students set topics to talk about. This might include topics or grammar or vocabulary they have recently learned in class, or it might be something from recent headlines or other big news stories.

Diplomacy

1 Group students in threes.

Student A and Student B must sit in different parts of the room. Student C will act as a go-between.

2 Give Student A a simple question. You could give every Student A in the class the same question, or the questions could be varied.

Choose your own question/s or choose from the suggestions below:
- What do you want for dinner tonight?
- Can we catch the bus home together after class?
- Can I borrow your favourite dress / shoes / shirt as I am going out on a date tonight?
- Can I borrow your dog to impress my new girlfriend / boyfriend?
- Can I stay at your place for two weeks?
- Can I borrow your car for the weekend?
- Will you ask your sister / brother out on a date with me?
- Will you help me go shopping for a new _____ tomorrow?

3 Student A tells Student C what his / her request is.

4 Student C must then go to Student B and tell Student B, as accurately as possible, what the request is.

5 Student B must give an answer to Student C, who then relays the answer to Student A, as accurately as possible. Student C, relaying each answer, may be involved in some negotiating between the Students A and B.

6 Student A then replies, and the reply is relayed to Student B, by Student C.

Student C may wish to write down each reply he / she relays.

Student A and B may wish to write down their own replies, or the replies of the other student, as the activity progresses.

7 This exchange continues back and forth until the activity becomes boring, or a time limit is reached, or a maximum number of exchanges is achieved.

Alternate activity

• Ask students to issue instructions for a task. These instructions should be relayed rather than questions and responses.

Feeling Your Way #1

1 Organise the furniture in the classroom into an obstacle course. This includes chairs, tables, even the teacher's desk if you have one. You could also use students' bags, folders, papers, etc: just make sure your course is not dangerous!

2 Put students in pairs.

3 Tell Student A to close his / her eyes. (Or you could use a handkerchief or an article of clothing for a blindfold.)

Tell Student A to verbally guide Student B through the obstacle course by giving instructions. Student A could be at Student B's side while they do this, or could give the instructions from the side of the classroom.

You could either ask the other pairs to leave the room while each pair works their way through the course, or you could change the obstacle course for each pair, or between every Student A and Student B.

4 The winner (if you want one) is the pair who completes the course in the shortest time, which you could time using your watch, or you could ask a student to time them.

Alternate activity

- Place things throughout the obstacle course that students need to pick up and collect. These could be the pens, papers, etc, or other things found in the classroom.

Feeling Your Way #2

1 Put students in pairs.

Place both students in chairs, back to back.

2 Tell Student A to close his / her eyes. (You could use a handkerchief or an article of clothing for a blindfold instead.)

3 Place an article in the open hands of Student A, something you have found in the classroom – a pen, a ruler, a book, anything.

4 Student A must describe how the article feels without saying what he / she thinks the article actually is.

As Student A speaks, Student B writes down the clues the article Student A is describing.

Decide on a time limit, or number of clues.

5 Swap so that each Student B cannot see, and must now describe how an article feels, while Student A writes.

Make sure you also swap articles between different pairs though, so that each pair is now describing and writing about an article new to them.

6 After both students are finished, they reveal what they think the article is.

Alternate activity

- Instead of writing down what the other student is saying, students draw the article being described.

Favourite Plot

1 Put students in pairs.

Tell Student A to think of the plot of a favourite film. But Student A cannot tell Student B what the name of the film is!

2 While Student A describes the plot of this film, Student B takes notes. Student A may also include the main actors of the film or any other personnel involved in the film, if he or she wishes. But don't reveal the title!

3 Students then swap, so Student B now describes the plot of a film while Student A takes notes.

4 Students re-form as a class, and taking turns, still without revealing the title of the film, all talk from their notes about the film their partner likes.

5 The winner is the classmate who guesses the most correct films. They may have to write these down as they go, to prove just who the winner is!

Alternate activity

• Instead of a favourite film, students talk about a favourite TV show.

Looking Out the Window

** This activity will only work if your classroom has a window that looks out onto a street or place where there is some activity happening.

1 Ask the student with the best listening skills to stand beside the window and look at what is happening outside.

2 Ask him / her to describe to the class what is happening outside.

3 Ask the rest of the class to listen and write down what is happening, as the first student speaks.

4 If there is a lot of constant action happening outside, you could repeat this activity with other students doing the describing.

Otherwise, you could repeat this exercise on other days with other students doing the describing.

Alternate activities

• If you have many windows or large windows, put students in pairs, and they take turns in either role.

• If you have a larger class, you could put students in small groups and run the activity with one student doing the describing and three or four or five students listening and writing. Groups could take turns at the window, or if there are many windows, run all the smaller groups at the same time.

• You as the teacher could also describe the action, as the whole class writes.

Homophonomania

1 Put students in pairs. One is Student A, while the other is Student B

Tell students you will read them a list of words and after each word, you will pause while Student A thinks up a sentence that includes the word, and says that sentence aloud.

2 Once Student A has thought up this sentence and said it, Student B must write the sentence down.

3 (While you are reading the words, if students ask which meaning is correct (meet or meat, allowed or aloud), tell them to make their own choice.)

4 Read the list for Student A first, then read the list for Student B.

Student A's List	Student B's List
meet	your
blue	their
right	caught
shoe	hour
feet	allowed

5 After students have finished writing their sentences, remind them what <u>homophones</u> are: words that sound exactly the same, but have different meanings and are spelled differently.

6 Tell students you are going to read them a list of words again. Read them this second list, which in fact are all the homophones from the first list.

7 Read the list for Student A first, then read the list for Student B.

Student A's ListStudent B's List
meatyou're
blewthere
writecourt
shooour
feataloud

8 And then tell students you have an extra word for them both:
they're

9 If you want a winner, it would be the students with the most sentences with the words used correctly.

Extra activity

• More homophones you could use to extend this activity include:

- where / wear
- hear / here
- flew / flue / 'flu
- four / for / fore
- maze / maize

… and there are many others

Superlative BINGO!

** This activity uses adjectives <u>and</u> adverbs.

1 Draw the chart below on the whiteboard:

Adjective	Comparative	Superlative	Adverb
		the saddest	
amusing			
			badly
		the most humorous	
	more interesting		
		the best	
	quieter		
			comfortably
lazy			
			helpfully

2 Tell students they must draw the same chart as you have.

3 Tell students you will read out the following words and they must write them in the correct spaces:

sadder	most comfortable	quietly
lazier	more amusing	humorous
most interesting	better	humorously
well	sad	more comfortable
most helpful	helpful	more humorous
good	interesting	bad
most amusing	comfortable	sadly
more helpful	lazily	worse
quiet	laziest	interestingly
worst	amusingly	quietest

4 Once you have read out all 30 words and all spaces have been filled, go through the answers as per below. To ensure all words are spelled correctly, you could write the answers on the whiteboard instead. Students could mark each other's work as you do so.

Adjective	Comparative	Superlative	Adverb
sad	sadder	the saddest	sadly
amusing	more amusing	the most amusing	amusingly
bad	worse	the worst	badly
humorous	more humorous	the most humorous	humorously
interesting	more interesting	the most interesting	interestingly
good	better	the best	well
quiet	quieter	the quietest	quietly
comfortable	more comfortable	the most comfortable	comfortably
lazy	lazier	the laziest	lazily
helpful	more helpful	the most helpful	helpfully

5 The student with the most correct answers out of 30 is the winner.

Alternate activity

• Here are some more adjectives and adverbs you could use instead:

Adjective	Comparative	Superlative	Adverb
fashionable	more fashionable	the most fashionable	fashionably
beautiful	more beautiful	the most beautiful	beautifully
warm	warmer	the warmest	warmly
brave	braver	the bravest	bravely
magnificent	more magnificent	the most magnificent	magnificently
delicious	more delicious	the most delicious	deliciously
cool	cooler	the coolest	coolly
angry	angrier	the angriest	angrily
light	lighter	the lightest	lightly
odd	odder	the oddest	oddly

Cooking BINGO!

** This activity works well with students who have to cook for themselves or will have to soon.

1 Tell students you will read the following list of words aloud. They will need to write them down.

add	chop	grate	prepare
bake	coat	grease	reduce
baste	combine	grill	remove
beat	cool	heat	roast
blend	cover	mash	roll
boil	cut	melt	rub
broil	fold	mix	sautée
chill	fry	peel	separate

simmer	squeeze	toast	warm
slice	steam	top	wash
spoon	stir	toss	whisk

2 Ask students which words they do not know the meaning of, and teach them these meanings.

3 Tell students to choose 22 (or half) of the words they wrote, and write these down on a separate list.

4 Tell them you will now read aloud the Method, from some recipes.

When they hear words they have chosen for their list of 22, they must cross the words out.

The first person to cross all the words out on their list and yell *BINGO!* is the winner.

You will need to read the recipes slow enough for students to hear the words, as they come fairly frequently.

Note: you should not come to the end of the sentences.

5 Check the list is correct once the first person yells *BINGO!*

Method:

Peel then chop the onions.

Sautée in butter then toss in sesame seeds.

Wash lettuce leaves then squeeze lemon juice over them.

Slice the potatoes and bring to the boil.

Cover and reduce to a simmer until tender, then mash.

Grate cheese over it and top with chives.

Prepare the other vegetables by cutting them into strips, then fry or steam them.

You can broil or grill the meat but a tastier version is: roll the meat in egg, then coat the meat with breadcrumbs.

Heat the oven for ten minutes, then roast for two hours.

Make sure you baste with the juices every thirty minutes.

Remove from the oven when it is cooked, and keep warm while you serve the vegetables.

Separate the egg whites from the yolks.

Whisk the egg whites, slowly adding the sugar, until stiff peaks form.

Fold the yolks into the egg whites.

Combine all the dry and wet ingredients, and blend for two minutes.

Melt the chocolate mixture then spoon into the pastry case.

Allow to cool slightly, then beat in the crushed almonds.

Chill in the fridge.

Rub the butter into the flour and sugar, then stir in the milk. Mix well.

Grease a cake tin and bake for 30 minutes.

Toast for a minute in the griller.

Extra activity

• Below is a list of more advanced verbs. Read them out in the order below, working down the columns. Students must write them down as you read them out.

barbecue	cream	garnish	pat
bone	crumble	glaze	place
burn	cube	halve	poach
catch	drizzle	lift	quarter
char	dust	lower	salt
core	freeze	mince	season
set	sift	strain	thicken
shake	skim	stuff	tie
shave	skin	sweeten	truss
shred	spice	tenderise	whip
sieve	stew	thaw	wrap

Ask students to pick 22 (or half) of them and rewrite as another list.

Read the shuffled list below, for another BINGO! Game.

The first person to cross all the words out on their list and yell *BINGO!* is the winner.

Check the list is correct once the first person yells *BINGO!*

barbecue	thicken	sweeten	cube
catch	spice	tenderise	tie
sift	bone	mince	stew
burn	shred	pat	wrap
cream	glaze	crumble	set
freeze	halve	poach	char
dust	lower	salt	shave
skim	strain	lift	place
garnish	drizzle	shake	sieve

quarter   stuff   thaw   whip

skin   core   season   truss

BINGO! for any Topic

1 Choose a topic you know is of interest to your students: sport, food, hobbies, anything. You could even choose grammar points or new vocabulary.

Brainstorm words about this topic on the whiteboard. Aim for 40 words.

2 Tell students to choose 20 of them and tell them to write the words down on their paper.

3 Work through the list of words on the whiteboard. Choose them randomly, not in order, and cross them out as you go.

The first person to cross all the words out on their list and yell BINGO! is the winner.

4 Check the list is correct once the first person yells BINGO!

Phrasal Verb Mix 'n' Match

1 Draw a line down the middle of the whiteboard, and write the heading <u>Phrasal Verbs</u>, as per the diagram below.

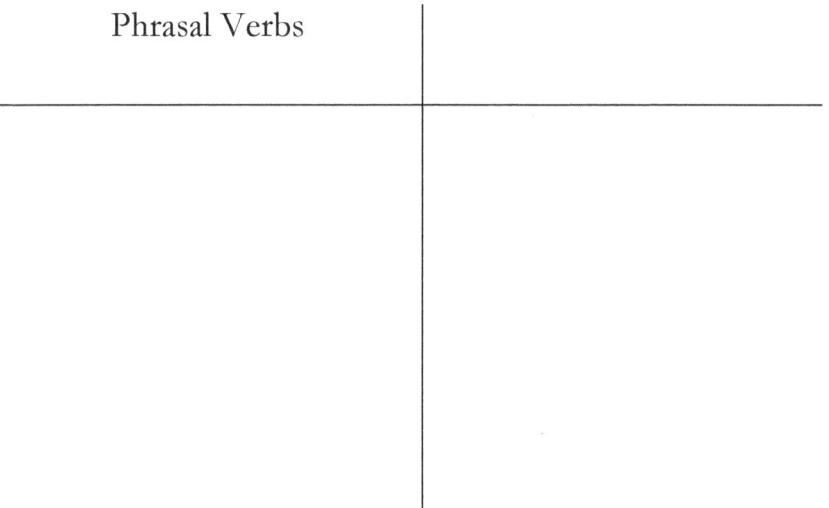

Phrasal Verbs

2 Ask students to explain what phrasal verbs are. Remind them they are a verb followed by one or more prepositions.

3 Tell students you are going to read out a list of verbs, and they must write them down under the heading <u>Phrasal Verbs</u>.

mix up	talk over	wrap up	take up
cut off	ring up	laugh off	count on
look up to	set off	take away	drop off
sum up	look over	set up	let down
crack up	look up	get up	work through

4 Ask students to organise the phrasal verbs in alphabetical order. Students can either do this individually, or you can do this as a class together on the whiteboard, as per the diagram below. Whichever process you choose, write the words on the whiteboard yourself. You will be able to correct spelling mistakes as you go.

Phrasal Verbs		
count on	mix up	
crack up	ring up	

cut off	set off
drop off	set up
get up	sum up
laugh off	take away
let down	take up
look over	talk over
look up	work through
look up to	wrap up

5 Tell students to write the heading <u>Formal Verbs</u> (as per the chart below). Then tell them you are going to read out another list of verbs, and they must write these down under this second heading on their paper.

confuse	disappoint	depart	laugh
depend	discuss	establish	summarise

find	dismiss	remove	interrupt
telephone	finish	rise	deliver
peruse	complete	start	respect

6 On the right side of the whiteboard at the top, write the words <u>Formal Verbs</u>. Ask the students to organise this second list into alphabetical order, as you chose to with the first list, as per the chart below. Again you can take care of any spelling issues as you go.

<u>Note</u>: a number of these phrasal verbs have multiple meanings, not all of which are included here.

Phrasal Verbs		Formal Verbs	
count on	mix up	complete	finish
crack up	ring up	confuse	interrupt
cut off	set off	deliver	laugh
drop off	set up	depart	peruse
get up	sum up	depend	remove

laugh off	take away	disappoint	respect
let down	take up	discuss	rise
look over	talk over	dismiss	start
look up	work through	establish	summarise
look up to	wrap up	find	telephone

7 Match the words on the left with their more formal counterparts on the right.

You could do this either by first identifying the words on either side that students have already heard or know the meaning of, or by working through the list on the left and crossing out the words on the right, as you go.

Or, students could match the verbs individually or in pairs, then these can be fed back to the class.

8 You may need to explain when to use phrasal verbs (everyday speech) and when to use more formal verbs (reports, speeches, etc).

Extra activity

• Students write sentences using phrasal verbs and their more formal counterparts, and identify the situations when they would use either version.

Human Dictionary

1 Write the words listed below on the whiteboard. Tell students they must write the words down also.

appear (v)	experience (v)
output (n)	enormous (adj)
falsely (adv)	vital (adj)
distant (adj)	partly (adv)
pattern (n)	turncoat (n)
consider (v)	exact (adj)
newsagent (n)	washable (adj)
statement (n)	experiment (v)

2 Tell students you are going to read out the meanings of all these words. All the meanings are listed below.

Students can either
(1) match the words with their meanings as you read them out and they write them down, or

(2) they can write them down now, and match them after the meanings have all be written down.

This matching could be done individually or in pairs or as a class.

(1) Not completely

(2) Huge, extremely large

(3) A decorative design, that you find on wallpaper, fabric or china

(4) A declaration in speech or writing

(5) Precise, and not approximate

(6) Dishonestly

(7) To participate in or undergo

(8) Able to be washed

(9) To become visible

(10) Far away, not close by

(11) The owner or manager of a business where you buy newspapers and magazines

(12) To try or test something, so that you can prove something or discover something about it

(13) The production or goods produced in a factory or business or by a person

(14) A person who stops supporting a particular group or opinion and joins an opposing group or changes opinion

(15) To think carefully about something so you can make a decision

(16) Of critical importance

3 Read out the answers below.

Answers:

appear (v)
(9) To become visible

output (n)
(13) The production or goods produced in a factory or business or by a person

falsely (adv)
(6) Dishonestly

distant (adj)
(10) Far away, not close by

pattern (n)
(3) A decorative design, that you find on wallpaper, fabric or china

consider (v)
(15) To think carefully about something so you can make a decision

newsagent (n)
(11) The owner or manager of a business or shop where you buy newspapers and magazines

statement (n)
(4) A declaration in speech or writing

experience (v)
(7) To participate in or undergo

enormous (adj)
(2) Huge, extremely large

vital (adj)
(16) Of critical importance

partly (adv)
(1) Not completely

turncoat (n)
(14) A person who stops supporting a particular group or opinion and joins an opposing group or changes opinion

exact (adj)
(5) Precise, and not approximate

washable (adj)
(8) Able to be washed

experiment (v)
(12) To try or test something, so that you can prove something or discover something about it

Alternate activity

• Ask students to contribute words to the list themselves. Write these on the whiteboard as they are called out.

Students then contribute the meanings to these words. Make sure, of course, that individual students aren't contributing meanings / answers to the words they have called out themselves.

Seasonal Activity

1 Write the following headings at the top of the whiteboard:
Winter / Spring / Summer / Autumn* / Don't Know
(* or Fall)

Tell students to write the same on their own paper.

2 Tell students you are going to read out of list of adjectives and they must write these words under the correct season. There may be more than one season for some of the adjectives.

If they do not know which season to put a word under, then include it under <u>Don't Know</u>.

steamy	ablaze	showery
fresh	crackling	freezing
balmy	hot	rotting
lazy	bare	sticky
green	close	falling
dry	new	growing

stinking	sunburned	orange
dying	red	humid
emerging	sweltering	warm
sunny	bitter	morose
icy	bleak	yellow
hopeful	thundery	stormy
long	sweaty	scorching
snowy	bleached	pleasant
endless	brisk	wet
happy	rainy	tired
foggy	clammy	cloudy
grey	frigid	cold
depressing	welcome	dead
frosty	cool	blistering

3 Once you have read out all of the words, ask the students if they wrote any under <u>Don't Know</u>.

If they did, work through their meanings and allow students time to slot them under the correct headings … or the headings that are correct for them.

4 Then work through the list of words, beginning with steamy and ending with blistering, placing them under the appropriate headings.

Where students write the words will depend upon cultural and geographical background, and could prove interesting and lead to class discussion

Alternate activity

• Make up a similar list of adjectives for emotions instead. You could draw a sad face, happy face, worried face and confused face on the whiteboard, and beside these a question mark for Don't Know.

About the Author

Matt Potter is an Australian-born writer who keeps part of his psyche in Berlin. He has worked as a social worker in Australia, in way too many jobs and sectors to mention, and as an English as a Second Language teacher in Australia and Germany.

Vestal Aversion (Pure Slush Books), his first collection of short stories, was published in 2012, and his memoir about living in Germany – *Hamburgers and Berliners and other courses in between* – was published in August 2015 by Červená Barva Press.

Based on True Stories, his second short story collection, was published in April 2016 by Truth Serum Press.

Find out a little more about Matt and his writing at his website http://mattcpotter.webs.com.

Also by Matt Potter from Everytime Press

all you need is ... a whiteboard, a marker and this book! Book 2

ISBN: 978-1-925101-96-6

- Speaking, Writing and Listening activities for English as a Second Language teachers who don't have any other resources at hand.
- An excellent resource when a teacher has been called in to teach and hasn't had time to prepare a thing!
- Fun and amusing activities bringing students' own lives and opinions into the classroom.
- Each activity includes alternate or extra activities.
- No other technology required beyond a whiteboard, a marker and this book!

Order it here:
http://www.everytimepress.com/apps/webstore/

About Everytime Press

We're a small but committed group of editors, publishers and writers with experience in independent / boutique publishing. We're interested in bringing to life smaller manuscripts that deserve publication but given their smaller size (132 trade-size pages minimum), find it hard to find a home with other presses.

We're committed to print, but embrace eBooks too.

We're looking for teaching resources, learning texts, memoir, travel and other non-fiction.

We're interested in working with writers who are not afraid to promote their own work, enjoy promoting their own work, and are creative when promoting their own work.

If you think we may be interested in your idea or manuscript, please email editor@everytimepress.com

Visit Everytime Press at
http://www.everytimepress.com

Visit the Everytime Press online store at
http://www.everytimepress.com/apps/webstore/

www.ingramcontent.com/pod-product-compliance
Lightning Source LLC
Chambersburg PA
CBHW020804160426
43192CB00006B/436